# EASY-TO-DRAW

# MYTHICAL CREATURES

by Mattia Cerato & Brenda Sexton

PICTURE WINDOW BOOKS
a capstone imprint

# MATERIALS

Before you start your amazing drawings, there are a few things you'll need.

pencil

colored pencils

markers

paper

eraser

ruler

# SHAPES

Drawing can be easy! If you can draw these simple letters, numbers, shapes, and lines, YOU CAN DRAW anything in this book.

**letters**

D S L U
V Z

**numbers**

1 2 3

**shapes**

**lines**

## OGRE

## UNICORN

## ELF

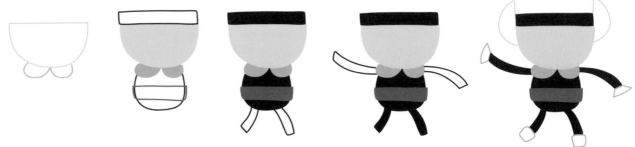

# CUPCAKE FAIRY

# WARRIOR PRINCESS

## GOBLIN

## FAUN

## DWARF

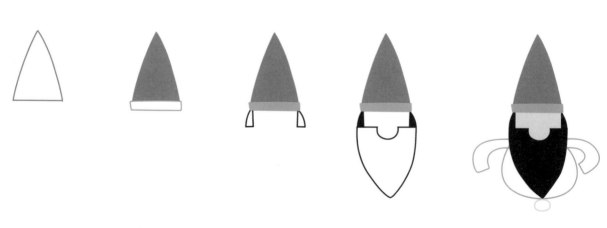

**Now try this!**

# FUTURISTIC PRINCESS

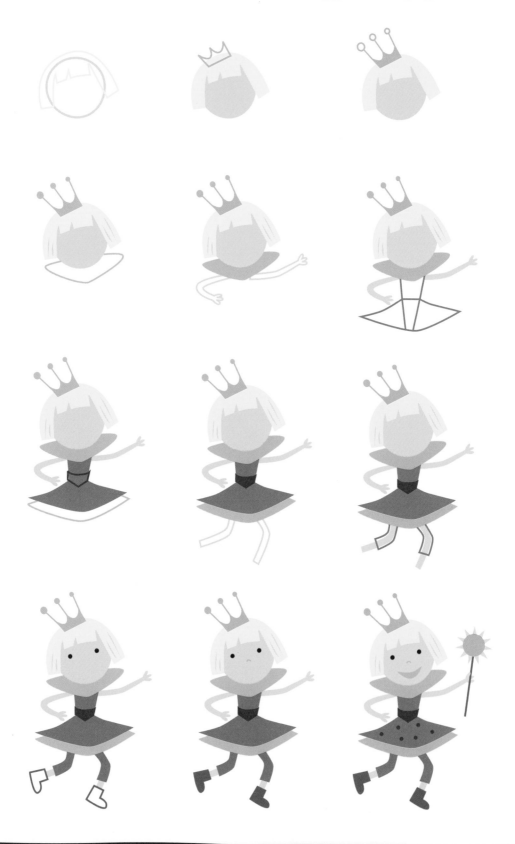

# BUTTERFLY FAIRY

# WIZARD

# TROLL

# CENTAUR

12

# PIRATE PRINCESS

Now try this!

# BUMBLEBEE FAIRY

# DRAGON

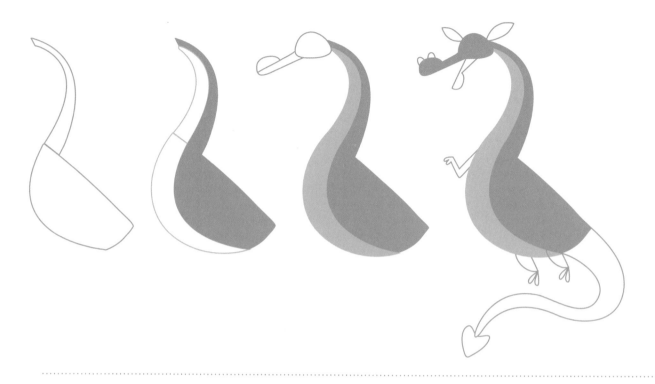

# GIANT

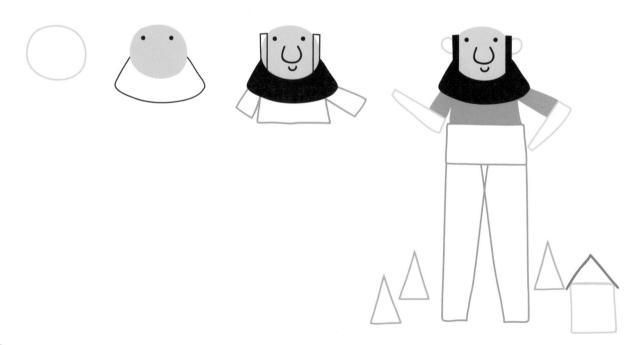

# STARDUST FAIRY

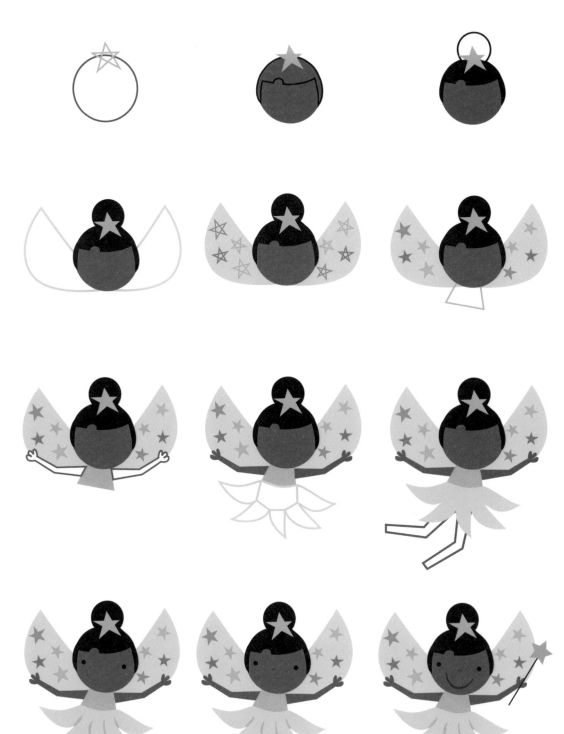

# ICE PRINCESS

## GRIFFON

## BABY DRAGON

## PEGASUS

## MERMAID

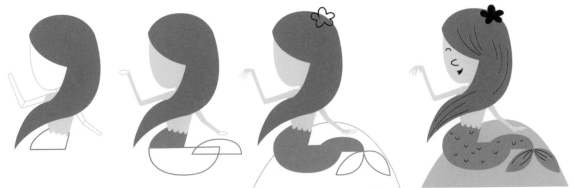

# EGYPTIAN PRINCESS

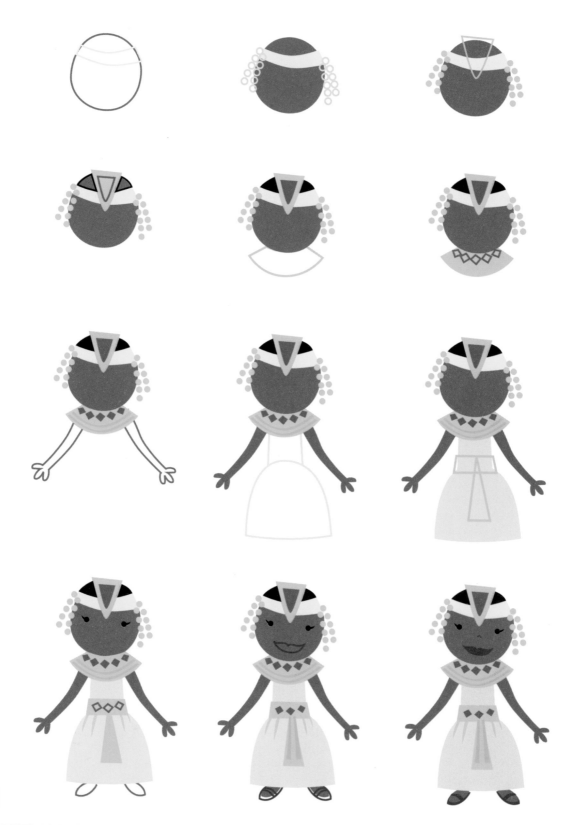

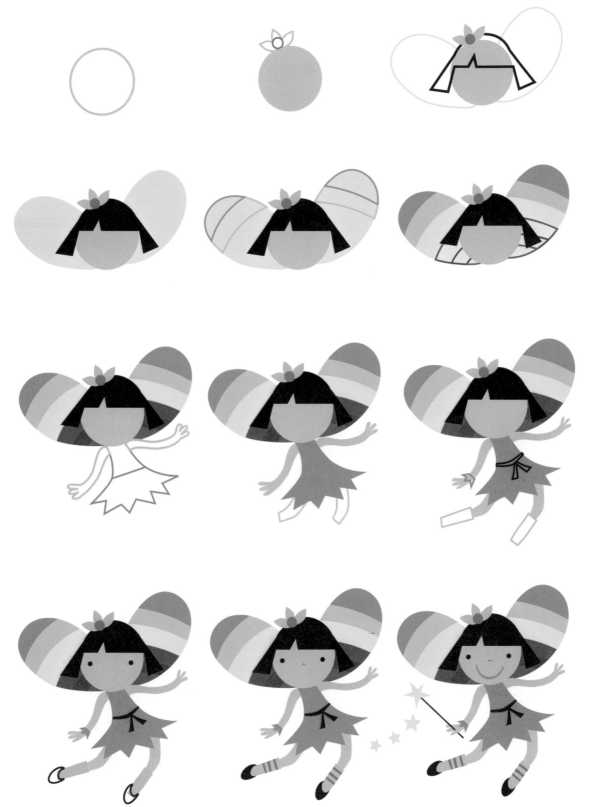

## THREE-HEADED SNAKE

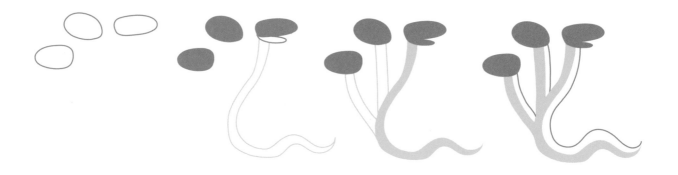

## WITCH

## CYCLOPS

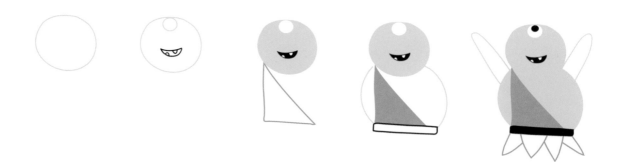

25

# NIGHTMARE FAIRY

# ALIEN PRINCESS

# MERMAN

# MEDUSA

# CERBERUS

Now try this!

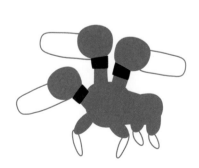

# CANDY PRINCESS

Now try this!

# TOOTH FAIRY

# MINOTAUR

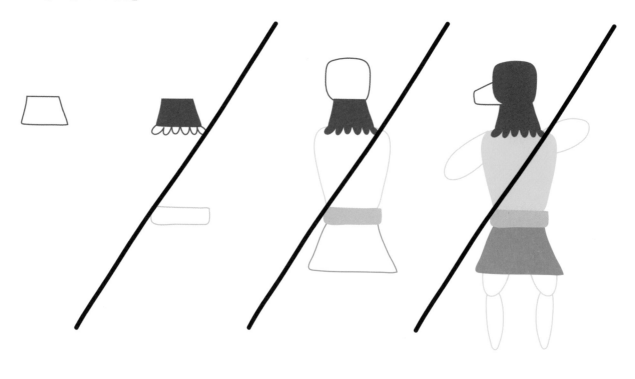

# PHOENIX

# BOOK FAIRY

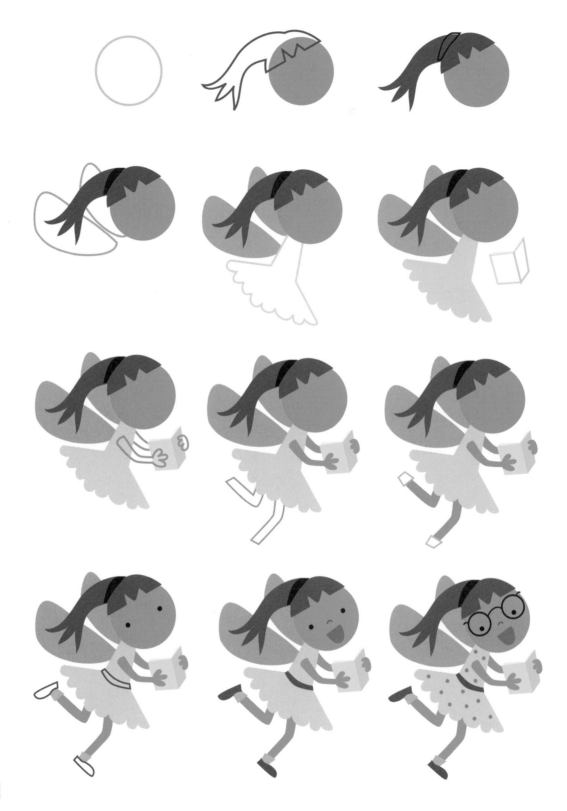

# EVIL PRINCESS

NOW THAT YOU'VE DRAWN ALL THE FAIRIES, PRINCESSES, AND CREATURES,

STIR THE POT BY ADDING SOME MAGICAL PROPS. ABRACADABRA! WHAT DO YOU GET?

A SPELLBINDING GOOD TIME!

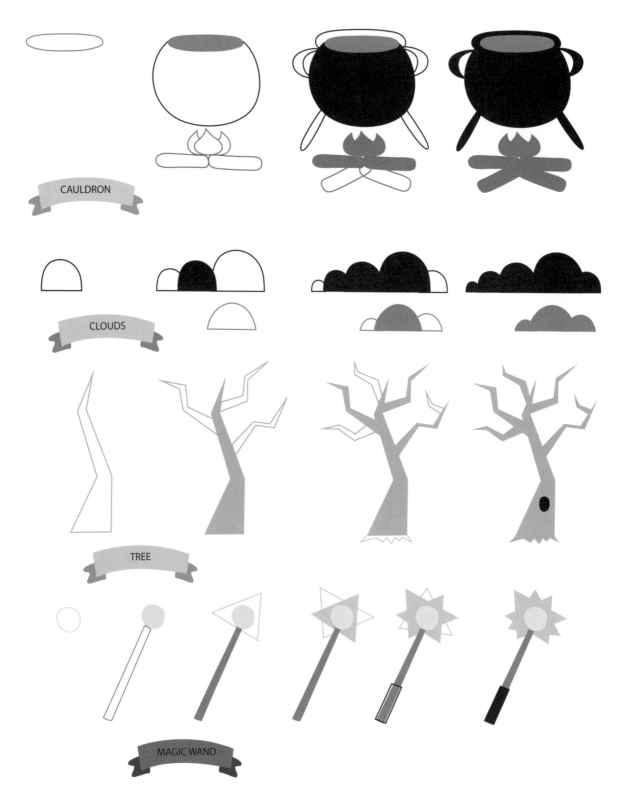

CAULDRON

CLOUDS

TREE

MAGIC WAND

CASTLE

MOUNTAINS

HILLS

CAVE

LIGHTNING BOLT

39

## BIRD

## TOOTHBRUSH

## VASE

# SILVERWARE

# TEAPOT

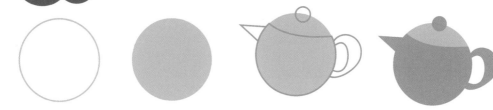

# GINGERBREAD MAN

# CAKE

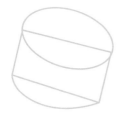   

# About the Authors

Mattia Cerato was born in Cuneo, a small town surrounded by the beautiful Italian Alps. Besides eating a lot of pasta at the age of 2 or 3, Mattia was introduced to drawing by his father, an artist in his own right. As a result he spent most of his time creating funny images on every surface he could find. When Mattia grew up, he decided to study illustration at the European Institute of Design in Turin, Italy. Within eight months of graduation, he started being represented by the MB Artists of New York City, and ever since then he's illustrated a lot of books. Mattia resides in Turin. When not illustrating, he enjoys playing basketball, traveling around the world, playing his bass guitar, and skiing in the Alps.

Brenda Sexton wishes she could live inside the colorful illustration world she creates. She has been honored for her whimsical illustrations by the Society of Children's Book Writers and Illustrators. She has also won four Emmy Awards for her work in sports television. Brenda lives and finds inspiration in the sunny California beach town of Marina Del Rey. Visit her at brendasexton.com.

Picture Window Books
151 Good Counsel Drive
P.O. Box 669
Mankato, MN 56002-0669
877-845-8392
www.capstonepub.com

Editor: Shelly Lyons
Designers: Matt Bruning and Tracy Davies
Art Director: Nathan Gassman
Production Specialist: Sarah Bennett
The illustrations in this book were created digitally.

Library of Congress Cataloging-in-Publication Data
Cataloging-in-publication information is on file with the Library of Congress.
ISBN 978-1-4048-7059-8

Printed in China.
072011        006314